NAKED THOUGHTS

Under The Silk Sheet

ELIAN ROXAN

Introduction

She start believing her self and wandered
what life would be like; allowing her confidence to take
control; to fixed what is broken. Most of us thinks
nonstop at midnight; useless things, future plans, great
things, steamy, erotic and a fairytale dreams we all love
to magically happen but sometimes this round earth
won't let it; so we leave it just a dream untill the very
end.

This poetry book is her way of showing of how
writing can heal and help forget of what hurts inside; of
 how every human minds and thoughts can scribbled the
emotions, the rides of life, moments and memories in a
sheet of paper; that in this unfair world their's magic and
we are worthy of love in every way, perhaps readers
might be moved by this book and write their own
 poetry.

Contents

little wild love
a
reason to stay

Naked Thoughts

And I sleep to dream
In this nude silk sheets
I hear him calling
the name I knew; even I closed my eyes
seductive whispers
our stars have come aligned
among the mess and the chaos
I love it; in the bed
with his open arms
and citrus smells
cause this is the beautiful place to start
and this is how we fall in love

Under the nude silk sheet of mine

Naked Thoughts

Tracing my curves
and contour it with reverence
his legs holding mine
in place my arms over my head
he sevours my taste
exalting in my warm
wet depths
noises escape my lips
it was heaven on earth
so intoxicating
I don't want it to end
a bruising desire
I can't even resist

Naked Thoughts

Craving for one night of a sin
waiting for you to sink
deep inside me
while you whisper
and I scream
kiss every inch of it
in the dimly lit cabin
making heavens
begging
for rain

Naked Thoughts

Your addictive love
and your immature tongue
making wave
in an intimate space
screaming your name
like nobody else
set me on fire
grooving until the end

Naked Thoughts

Summer nights
I can feel the heat
dimmed light smooth jazz
the wild silence in your eyes
savoring me with such devotion
causing me to grin
growls like a wild wolf
please
let be like this until
the winter night

Naked Thoughts

You trace the skin along my back
shoulder to shoulder
spine to spine
your hands fitting mine
whispered in my ears
all those promises
our eyes met
we make love
of this moment
echoes of the night
light up the skies

Naked Thoughts

HE lays me in his bed
spread my legs
I love the way HE make me beg
showered my beauty
His eyes capture my femininity
wetting his lips before HE tasted
worshiping me wildly
Sipping my eternity
witnessing the devine
unaware of the holy light
the wildest love
there's a reward
an endless sea
drowned by your love

Naked Thoughts

The desire races through my veins
every kiss, suck and bite.
Every trace of his tongue
rolling down the hill
glided over the edge
as his hand play melodies
taking control
firing my soul

Naked Thoughts

Kisses on my neck

eyes full of lust

his skin againts mine

savouring sweet clam

bodies bent over the chair

making love in the shower

over flowing desire

made her wet

dripping down to her legs

magic of love

we both made a habit

Naked Thoughts

Morning cuddle
that lead to sex
surprised as we go for a ride
sweet breath
chest is rising
tracing my thighs
with your finger tips
pure ecstasy
imposible to quite
the morning cuddle
I don't want to end

Be my melody
in this
music sheet

Naked Thoughts

She is
emotionally unsure
the thorns surrounding her
keep on growing
softly touching the delicate white roses
turning into bloody red.

Someone
is talking to
SHE
about the dark tunnel
without end.

Beautiful brown brow
without eyes.

She remember
everything
but
She didn't see
anything.

Naked Thoughts

Chasing the last summer, fall and winter.
I love rainy days and the spring with your blooming
 gaze. Feeling happy in every moment, sharing sunset
and my coconut drinks; how magical it is, that makes
me want to kiss you in every season; taste you in my
tongue like every love song, undress your body and
undress your soul.

Naked Thoughts

She is inlove with sunday
wrapped in blankets
with pillow on her legs
her lazy ass
in her safe haven
listening to Rachmaninoff
dancing in her dream.
Her curly hair touching
her nose tip
lying in bed naked

Oh

I so love you
Sunday

Naked Thoughts

Our goodbye is on repeat
like a parrot in the golden cage
I missed you word
"Text me when you get home safe"
your 3:00 AM call
even I am naked
I wish to end
our goodbyes that on repeat
to a fairy tale
with a

Happy End

Naked Thoughts

I did love you
do you understand me?

I was standing there
waiting for you to pick me

I did love you
do you understand me?

So much
that I let you destroy me

I did love you
do you understand me ?

I am no longer me
but I did love you

and my heart
is beating for you

do you understand me?

Naked Thoughts

I see no sparkle in your eyes
nor dream in your heart
you did stop looking
for the rainbow
you curse the fate
blame somebody else
you wish to disappear
in this world
full of fear

Naked Thoughts

Yesterday I am alone
today I am more alone
I have accepted the situation
to sit with loneliness
embrace it as if it was a gift
to be more isolated.
I wish to wash my face
to untangle my self
to have a quescent day
In the outer space.

Naked Thoughts

Dandelion who dance in the wind
Have you fall Inlove
to a man in a faraway land?

--impatient to meet him--

Hush, Don't rush

He might walk through your life

In a eerie woods at night
you might see his sparkling eyes

Blows it
One
Two
Three

Make a wish a thousand times

perhaps

You'll meet him under the moonlight

Naked Thoughts

I am here for mature love
A love
that I can count on
A love
that I have enjoy every moment
A love
that isn't too great
but always stays
A love
which
is
Art

Naked Thoughts

I'm so tired of being lost
for trying to put this puzzle together
for trying to feed this soul
to water this heart
cause it's to painful to realize
that the alignment is diffucult
and that because
we all grow
at the different rates
that sometimes we chose sadness
instead of joy in softer moments

She is Art

Naked Thoughts

24

She dances until
she can dance no more
picking the rose
who have lost their red
even she's back
to nothingness
theirs the sand
that always wait
theirs the wave
clapping at it's own pace
and the sun
that rises
in the east

Naked Thoughts

Commited a sin to ends of the earth

For loving you
without loving my self
forgetting who I should love first

So
I just commited a sin

for leaving you
cause
I love

ME

and

MY SELF

Naked Thoughts

The darkness of the night
echoed in my heart
hoping to fall asleep
before I fall a part

Naked Thoughts

She was a poppy
in the greenest field
who bloomed beautifully
in the windy night
who dance
in the mystery
of madness
and sing like
a humming bird
born in the cycle of pain
where sun seems like would never shine
again
hoping to save this summer
because
it's just so warm.

Naked Thoughts

28

Going home alone
holding my selves
through storm
drinking the beauty
of love from afar
fearless woman
who find her self back
 into the wild

Naked Thoughts

She is the red hair queen
who lived in the unknown dream
she run in darkness
with her half naked soul
among the chaos and mess
she wanted to be saved

but no one did

Naked Thoughts

I wrote this poetry
to put the heart at ease; to make peace with my past
which heart bleeds in gloomy nights.

Naked Thoughts

she is cautious
with who she lets in
devine goddess
blossoming
into her wildest life
treasuring her self
like art
dancing
in the earth above

Naked Thoughts

Chaos swirls in her brain
tears of pain
lost in those sappire gems
she waltz around the truth that never told
doubting the other half of her soul
she chose to close her eyes
to see her silhouette
she can't recognize

Naked Thoughts

The days when its easier to drawn than to float

The sun behind the rain on a cloudy days

A voice sounded like earl gray tea

when smiling was free

but all we can hear is silent tears

It's another spring

behind the storm

Naked Thoughts

Red color
againts the night sky
she walked across the light
an illusion as if she was flying high.

The girl who have wings like butterfly
come down chasing the love instead of receiving
following his soul; chasing silently
but every step is a step
in the wrong direction.

I see no sparkle in her eyes
night have always been dark
no stars nor clouds.

It's a dark road
with her naked soul and bleeding scars.

A rare sight
that can only be seen in the dark

Naked Thoughts

The Princess of peaceful
A rebel
that never cross the line
A Goddess
who think deep
waited patiently
to cross under the broken bridge
The scars
with scary stories
which hidden
uder the white halo on her head

Naked Thoughts

We submitted to each others soul
my muse
who's poem
written on her body
trying to create words
with love, lust and romance
with her brown eyes
looking deep
in the universe
you can keep

Naked Thoughts

Perhaps what is broken
will not heal today

Perhaps you haven't figure things out yet

Perhaps you still struggling
with difficult things

girl you are not a failure
you have done your best atleast

so keep going
and smell the earth after the rain

Naked Thoughts

I can't wait to be happy
So I exhaust my self completely
I eat food that wasn't good
I walk in the wild
for me to get lost
I write a journal
with just fucking word
I sleep late
so that I can have a long deep sleep
I set boundaries
I shut down people

Oh! I can't wait to be happy

Naked Thoughts

I knew you for a long time
I met you for a short time
If only I could stop time
Us together would have been
lasted for a lifetime.

I wish to meet you again
one more time
to hold your hand
until we die.

Naked Thoughts

Hurts leak from your eyes
let your worries rest in my palms
let's dance in the lost melodies
especially when the tempo turn to slow
lose our self; shut the world out
let's be happy together
and look for our stars
in a small town.

Naked Thoughts

I spend my weekend
at the beach Chris

It's beautiful

the sea was beautiful

walking on the shore
wearing your old black hat

The sea is waving Chris

It's calling me
It's pulling me
I can't reason with it
I am losing my breathe

Chris

I might see you again
under the wave

Naked Thoughts

So busy chasing the distraction
So busy running through dark place
So busy clearing the path

standing on a subtle boundary

refusing to heal

I don't push it away

desperately waiting
Quietly urging

Naked Thoughts

Joy hidden in pain

Lonely soul
found in darkness

Unknown soundtract
to this beautiful life

Mother crows crying in silence

Throwing shinning diamond
in the well of heartache

Wishing wishes to be granted

On a soulful journey
in the hidden valley

Moans in my mouth

Lullabies to his ears

Naked Thoughts

My heart pumps
as you press your hips to mine
your lips sunburn my lips
moaning commences
we ride onto waves of sensation
making me weak
making me drunk
asking more
of your lust

Naked Thoughts

47

Calling your name
in sweet rhyme
sliding my finger
down to your spine
your everybreath is giving me life
so dramatic it's set us on fire
makes me realize
you make me so high

Naked Thoughts

Floating around in ecstasy
soul, heart and sexuality
silence my pretty little mouth
who moans slowly
ache for intimicy
tender and hard
he owns me completely
burried
in me
on me
until the sun rise

Naked Thoughts

Dancing in the rain
drench with you in this rhythm
pulling me closer
make me hungry for more
your lips trailing down my neck
yes, more...
lust dripping with desire
dancing with our soul

Naked Thoughts

A coffee
A pancake
A honey
and a butter
All this for later

first

I want a morning
sex

with you

Naked Thoughts

I am wet hot chili pepper

salted caramel
he remove my worries

sweet like honey
licking so gently

We sink

We fit

We're just ment to be
in this king size bed

Naked Thoughts

Bathed in the moonlight
rose petals
in midsummer night
mouth excites
in this heavenly flavor
swaying, licking her lips
tasting the salt on her skin
ignite a flame
to a sinful seen

Naked Thoughts

He pushed her
againts the wall
kissed her neck
put his hand
around her waist
he move his finger
to her curve
sliding in under
her red dress
he groaned
I moaned
ending it
to our sweet scape

Naked Thoughts

Sipping my coffee
wearing white tee
without undies.

In his eyes I fell
he slides his fingers
electrifying my inner.

A play date in the morning
in a white tub of heaven
those tiles feels cool hot chills
he've turned on the shower
his mouth between my legs
chalice of nectar are over flowing
lust and romance.

let me breath for a moment
so I can live with this moment
over and over
again and again.

Naked Thoughts

We discover each other as treasure
exploring each others body
bringing unending pleasure.

Touching the deepest part of our soul

Naked Thoughts

She longed to feel his warm hands
his lips at midnight

Fantasizing

Heart races
hardly catches my breath
his hands reach for me
hot and hungry

melts me

Naked Thoughts

57

He smelled like coffee
wakening my innerthing
makes me crave
for fantasies
with
love stories

Naked Thoughts

I thank her with a kiss on the neck
I'm going to start
fulfilling her request
I plan on hiking
with my tongue
through valleys of flesh
down to her earth

Flames around us
a
Burning desire

Naked Thoughts

Dancing with you in the kitchen
while my foot on your feet
my head on your chest
feeling your heartbeat
making most mundane moments
like fairytales

Dancing under the glazing stars
in the tune of love

Naked Thoughts

Tongue inviting the taste of dawn

flavorful salt at your finger tips

vanilla ice cream are melting down

coax my release

my lonesome mind

you set me on fire

Naked Thoughts

Calling our names across the constellation
sweet scent of summer rain
we bath under the moonlight
with infinite love
kissing my hand
you put a diamond ring
whispering softly
the lovely poetry

Naked Thoughts

Her smile is all illusion
where her body craves to be touched
kissed her under the stars
cause her beauty
is a work of art
so be with her tonight
fuck her till midnight
but love her for the rest of your life

Naked Thoughts

Waiting for the wrong breeze
to untie the forbidden verbs

Swallowing hate and corrodes
saturating syllables
I cannot pronouce

I am bewitched
as we coast along the flowery road

Admitting my feeling
dispelling everything

Photographing my beauty
pulling me to the world of poetry

Naked Thoughts

The day I spent with you
was bright
even the stormy day seems like
a sweet cotton candy cloud
embracing the art
created by your hand
dancing in the moonlight
where stars shines bright

Naked Thoughts

Be gentle as you touch my heart
spell my name with so much love
place your hand in my soul
as we sing desperately
at breaking dawn

Naked Thoughts

He touches my every soul
it echoes the eternity
let my body speak
threading each others ecstasy
moaning under the dark sky
intensely
loosing my mind

Naked Thoughts

Wine stains on my skin
heat start to rise
I feel your lips
I can feel your love
pulsates wildly inside
my hand raise to touch
mouth floods with wanting
a flood of desire
drench in wine
running through my vain

Naked Thoughts

This place is a sanctuary
bed full of roses
scream echoed in darkness
you stare in my silhouette
giving me a satisfaction
leaving trails of blisters
with no shame and hesitancy
another lost soul
found her perfect sanctuary

Naked Thoughts

He walk through my life
without blinking eyes

He made a paradise
in flaming white

He turn into snake

my lover who bite my limbs

licked the flesh

suck the honey

the dripping lust

he love to taste

The most beautiful

thing I knew was

YOU

Naked Thoughts

Love her
like if it's your last

Love her
like no one else does

Love her
co'z she was a diamond
who can brought spark to your life

Love her
until your black hair
turn into gray and white

Naked Thoughts

Choking me gently
I can't hardly breath
biting your lips
hot sauce sweet taste
desperately drawn
by your touch without direction
hunger is in your eyes
we had a sleepless night

Naked Thoughts

Falling inlove with my selves
sharing it to you
cause I also fall for you

I took my diary out
wrote down your name
cause I want you to stay

sitting on your lap

tasteful cake
you licked my finger tip

savouring your lips
it's just so sweet.

my selfish love wanted
you to stay.

Naked Thoughts

Visiting my hometown
I saw you for the first time
showed me your sweetest smile
and ask permission to hold hand
You ask
Are you naughty?
I said
No, but
I can be the sweetest devil
who need your body
giving both
pleasure and sweet serendipity

Naked Thoughts

Don't wear me as your regret

let it be love!

Don't undress me with your emotions

let it be love!

cause

I want to walk around

full of love

filled with your love

Naked Thoughts

The sun sets with hymn
welcoming the dark lullabies
hearing his voice
calling my name
calling my soul
releasing his desire
brightly like a star

Naked Thoughts

I'm trying to steal one more glimps
is it my lover who's trying to leave?
like fate that never meet
my mind keep wandering
was it you I saw in heaven?

or

Perhaps you were that dandelion
I saw
who dance in the wind.

Naked Thoughts

Dark
Strong
Hot
My lips wanted to touch
morning
afternoon
wanted you even at night
comforts me in rainydays
especially when no one else around
your aroma is a sun kissed to my heart
my coffee in a black cup
stay with me
in this cold night

Naked Thoughts

I wish to meet you once again
even the love was gone

I wish to meet you once again
to weep my happiest and saddest tears

I wish to meet you once again
before the death take me away

I wish to meet you once again
to be with you

and

to be loved by you

Naked Thoughts

Be my heaven
in this world full of storm and thunder

Be my heaven
even the volcanoes began erupting again

Be my Heaven
So I could call your name everyday

Be my heaven
In this dark rooms full of dreams

Naked Thoughts

82

You comfort all my worries
lick my every tears
leave me stunned
of how good of you
playing with this heart.
You pick me up
sit me on your lap
we're soaked in this passion
bathed in our lust

To be the only hand
you ever need to hold

Naked Thoughts

It's okay
to meet strangers
to give them a warm hand

It's okay
to ask the moon
even it covered by dark clouds

It's okay
to love him silently
even he loved somebody else

It's okay
just
listen to music
because
love would reach you
at the end

Naked Thoughts

She has a voice like a liquid gold
a child of the universe
who brought stars to my world
Her heart sings a song
in the hymns of lullabies
dancing in the tune
completing my life
turning it into
blossoming cherry blossom

Naked Thoughts

Her silken skin
burning eyes
she sit and watch
to the birds who flocked
on a little island
while she murmured in silent tears
she lost her dream
she lost her way
she lost everything

but

He came to save her soul

Naked Thoughts

When will I be worth the risk?

When will this heart be enough for another

When will I find someone

who would hold my hand
untill the rest of my life?

When it could be?

The time I could meet

HE...

Naked Thoughts

Joy soak into my skin
breathing in the magic of love
you watered the heart
that bloomed
in the abyss of time.
The smell of your french perfume
woke up the butterflies
flying under the blue skies
enchant my heart; my soul
feeling the liberation.
Converts my melancholy
to mystical moment.
This journey with you
will be worth it
in the end.

Naked Thoughts

He is a ten
Reg flags
I saw all the butterflies
Green flag
I saw love in his eyes
His smiles fluttering my heart
I can't stop looking
I can't stop dreaming

Naked Thoughts

I never wished on a shooting star
nor ask the moon
to bring back your heart

I never wished to be in the enchanted forest
so we could see faries
playing hide and seek

I never wished to change the weather every winter
so we could touch the morning dew
from the purple flower

I never wished to lost you in a dream
I never dreamt

Naked Thoughts

Planting the seeds of love
together we shall water them
how lovely it is;
to see the blooming heart.

Playing in the playgroud
you pushed the swing
along with my dream
pink petals were fallen;
catching it
cause it's the memories
we both shared.

Telling me stories
were both you and me are the leading
giggling; cause it's just so romantic

Washing my hair filled with love
caressing my heart

The unending love between us
I have wished to last

Naked Thoughts

You made my whole life
like it's my birthday

like a book of love
I keep it in my heart

Pure and real

filled with care

loving endlessly

like a lavander
wanted to bloom in winter

Naked Thoughts

This feeling is uncontrollable
like the first snowfall
subline and silence
communal soul escape
tracing his footprints
a snowball fight at the end
giggling heart I feel delighted
lost in paradise
I've got hypnotized
genuine love
in someones poetry
the well deserve love
looking for a life story

Naked Thoughts

94

He is a unicorn
a mythical creature
who exists in fairyland
who pulled me in the world
of raining heart
overwhelmed
at the purest gesture of him
saving my saddest heart
mesmerizing
from the beauty
of love.

Naked Thoughts

Mello harmonica
playing inside my heart
dancing in the sweet melody
with your warm embrace
fire works in the sky
I saw you smiling
lookin at my eyes
makes my heart
flutter all the time
clinging to music, to poems
to writing, to art
and to you
cause this is
another spring
in the tiny cabin

Find your love
in
every place

Naked Thoughts

Uncompromising battles
in the world which called universe
accepting the entropy
balancing force
between order and chaos
too many obstacles
too many enemies
because yourself
were loosing
the precious memories

naked thoughts

Flowers sprinkle with rain
fingers of flesh
scratches my neck
as you dance
like a flame in the dark
burned me with passion
awakens my soul
my desires

and

I am
here to
hunt

naked thoughts

The amount of ecstasy
from celestial
sunset skies
cool blues of peace
the yellow happiness
the tree waves
from unexpected
independence
calm and safe
keen for a warm embrace
flowers who understand
the people's words
which hearts hide an
untold story
remain unwritten
through history

naked thoughts

I hope were not 5000 miles away

It might be hard
but I want to seat next to you
while you're driving; to fit my finger through yours
while your left hand on the steering.

It might be hard
but I want to feel your arms
wrap around my waist; pulling me closer
to hear you whisper "I love making love to you all day".

It might be hard
but i want to fall for you even deeper
to stay with you forever.

It might be hard
but I hope were not
5000 miles away or further.

naked thoughts

Don't be a tease
You!
lady in red

I making love to you in my head
lured me in darkness

clench onto your hands
you kissed me
had me hypnotized

I welcome the hurt
only make me
desire for your lust

causes poetic mayhem
in my head

naked thoughts

This is from the heart of someone you hurt.
Someone who waited for you to be back
Someone who cried silently; even she smiled
Someone you starved for love
Someone you laugh at when
she's started to begged for little happiness
Someone who hope to get back;
even she was dying inside.
She so fucking love you
that she accepted the scars
and pretend that
she had none.

naked thoughts

I am still alive
I keep on fighting
trying to understand
everything
I wish to disappear
I wish I wasn't here
in a world full of fear
my mind goes numb
what are my future plan?
dreaming without a dream
tormenting feels
watching the glass shatter
I see blood everywhere
please take me out of here.

SAVE ME...

naked thoughts

I've spent my days
chasing after the sound
coffee shop chatters, taps on keyboard
tic tac of pen, click clack of heels
laughter of the unknown human
a life dilluted with distraction
till I realized; I was in bed alone.
Staring on my ceiling; was it falling?
clock is crying out loud; it's twelve midnight.
Creaky stairway of memories
chasing the happiness
in the dark room of attic.
Why the world aren't sleeping?
even the moon keep on talking
my body was shaking; stuck with my self
screaming with sadness.
A voice without words in darkness
asking for help.

naked thoughts

Sometimes
it's hard to find the reason to live

Sometimes
I just wanted everything to end

Sometimes
I hide so many things

to comfort my self
to comfort my soul

naked thoughts

I have never felt
the love again
after planting
the bed of roses
with his own hand
thorns keep digging
in my heart
its bleeding
it falls apart

naked thoughts

The first love I would never forget
even when pages turn it never seems end
looking back from the past
satisfying my heart
even it will hurt.

I keep coming back
allowing my self to be fooled.

It hurts
but
I won't mind
turning back to first page with brokenheart.

naked thoughts

The moon laugh and whispered
"In your eyes I see paradise"
she laughed, feels like holiday
she's carrying a heavy heart on silence.
The blooming flower stares at her as if facing the sun
every time she speaks,
the breeze blows and the sunflower vows
sharing thoughts with the universe
untangled the most mundane matters
serene and bright
an ordinary life beneath the wild sky
learning and forgetting
thinking the imperfection
dreaming of somebody else
even our love wasn't ment to be
in the unfinished tale in someone's poetry

Demon behind the window cracked
in a dark quite woods
looking at the empty sky
asking the moon
about his unwanted heart
counting days;
counting dreams
His frozen time;
unsaid thoughts
trying to fuel the dying world.
His dying soul
seared with scars
longing for something
he could never have.

naked thoughts

His eyes are my prison
paradise with his reflection
resting on his shoulder
thirsty for every inch of space on his heart.
The swelling of my heart
after he touch it
lured me into hypnotic sleep
such is love
I see in his eyes

naked thoughts

Perhaps love doesn't exist between us
Perhaps you wanna see me drunk
shouting your name to heal this broken heart
Perhaps this silent agony bearing the untold story
perhaps you wanna save this heart;
perhaps
Not?

naked thoughts

My morning black coffee
sliding down through my throat
warming my saddest heart.

Image stained in my mind
haunted by his deep desire

It's Monday
I watch him go
in a cracked window

I wake up in fear
calling his name

and

I didnt see him again
Monday after Monday

naked thoughts

I did not wait for friday
to see us run away to each other

I did not wait for friday
to dance in the beach without your feet

I did not wait for friday
to see the stars without you by my side

I did no wait for friday
to watch our favorite movie
but you are happier with her

I did not wait for friday
to end our story at the hallway

I did not wait for friday
to love you wholeheartedly
but you love her instead

naked thoughts

Dancing in the rain
free of pain and suffering

I think about you
undressing my tan skin

like a caterpillar
who thought the world was ending

It makes me wonder
when would this scars heal

naked thoughts

She is quite well versed
in playing with fears
She laugh while in tears
filled with passion, dread
and unspoken secrets
stayed in the dark
in silent night

naked thoughts

Behind those eyes
I see goodbyes
Unwillingly see
the rejection
of the universe offered
fragile heart of glass
pretending to be beast
Soft and fluffy
She was just a cotton candy
Sweet and tasty
she's just a honeybee

naked thoughts

Even the most admired masterpiece aren't perfect
they are often chaotic with different strokes
which gently strokes become blade and white roses turns red
just like the life you chased in a wrong pace.
As if there's no escape into a cycle of pain;
as if the sun would never shine again.
You might've ask your self how certain things happen.
Perhaps it should have been a joyous day in that poignant,
mundane every day moments.Why not chase the exquisite
sun that sets in the east and laugh with those poppy
who loved to dance in the windy field

naked thoughts

Tonight let me be your biggest sin
and your wildest dream

Catching stars
in my own universe

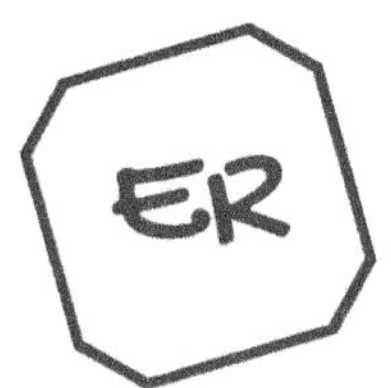